Blue Banner Biography

Ciara

Amie Jane Leavitt

Mitchell Lane
PUBLISHERS

P.O. Box 196
Hockessin, Delaware 19707
Visit us on the web: www.mitchelllane.com
Comments? email us: mitchelllane@mitchelllane.com

Mitchell Lane PUBLISHERS

Printing   1   2   3   4   5   6   7   8   9

Blue Banner Biographies

Akon	Alan Jackson	Alicia Keys
Allen Iverson	Ashanti	Ashlee Simpson
Ashton Kutcher	Avril Lavigne	Bernie Mac
Beyoncé	Bow Wow	Britney Spears
Carrie Underwood	Chris Brown	Chris Daughtry
Christina Aguilera	Christopher Paul Curtis	**Ciara**
Clay Aiken	Condoleezza Rice	Daniel Radcliffe
David Ortiz	Derek Jeter	Eminem
Eve	Fergie (Stacy Ferguson)	50 Cent
Gwen Stefani	Ice Cube	Jamie Foxx
Ja Rule	Jay-Z	Jennifer Lopez
Jessica Simpson	J. K. Rowling	Johnny Depp
JoJo	Justin Berfield	Justin Timberlake
Kate Hudson	Keith Urban	Kelly Clarkson
Kenny Chesney	Lance Armstrong	Lindsay Lohan
Mariah Carey	Mario	Mary J. Blige
Mary-Kate and Ashley Olsen	Michael Jackson	Miguel Tejada
Missy Elliott	Nancy Pelosi	Nelly
Orlando Bloom	P. Diddy	Paris Hilton
Peyton Manning	Queen Latifah	Ron Howard
Rudy Giuliani	Sally Field	Selena
Shakira	Shirley Temple	Tim McGraw
Usher	Zac Efron	

Library of Congress Cataloging-in-Publication Data
Leavitt, Amie Jane.
   Ciara / by Amie Jane Leavitt.
      p. cm. — (Blue banner biographies)
   Includes bibliographical references and index.
   ISBN 978-1-58415-610-9 (library bound)
   1. Ciara (Vocalist)—Juvenile literature. 2. Singers—United States—Biography—Juvenile
literature. I. Title.
ML3930.C47L43 2008
782.42164092—dc22
[B]   2007019789

ABOUT THE AUTHOR: Amie Jane Leavitt is the author of more than a dozen books for children. She has also written magazine articles, puzzles and games, workbooks, activity books, and tests for kids and teens. Ms. Leavitt is a former teacher who has taught many subjects and grade levels. She loves to travel, play tennis, and learn new things every day as she writes. She believes that everyone should follow his or her dreams.

PHOTO CREDITS: Cover—Frank Micellota/Getty Images; p. 4—Amanda Edwards/Getty Images; p. 7—Frederick M. Brown/Getty Images; p. 10—Scott Cunningham/Getty Images; p. 11—Erik S. Lesser/Getty Images; p. 15—Vince Bucci/Getty Images; p. 16—Michael Buckner/Getty Images; pp. 19, 21, 25—Kevin Winter/Getty Images; p. 23—Bryan Bedder/Getty Images.

PUBLISHER'S NOTE: The following story has been thoroughly researched, and to the best of our knowledge represents a true story. While every possible effort has been made to ensure accuracy, the publisher will not assume liability for damages caused by inaccuracies in the data and makes no warranty on the accuracy of the information contained herein. This story has not been authorized or endorsed by Ciara.

At age nineteen, Ciara Princess Harris recorded her first album. This achievement isn't something that came easy. Ciara worked diligently for years to accomplish this dream.

Goodies

*I*t was September 28, 2004. In less than one month, Ciara (see-AIR-uh) Harris would be turning nineteen years old. Yet that is not why this date is so special to this young woman. Ciara knew that in nearly every music store in town, a new CD was on display. It was titled *Goodies*, and it was Ciara's very first album! She couldn't believe that her dream of becoming a musician had actually come true.

Most likely, the calls to the Harris household started coming in like crazy that day. All their close friends and family would want to know every last detail of Ciara's good fortune. How did she feel about her new album? Was she excited? What would she do next? Would she be traveling on a national music tour or appearing on television soon?

Goodies was popular not only in Ciara's hometown of Atlanta, but it was also extremely popular around the country and the world. Released by LaFace Records, this album contained thirteen songs. Some of them featured other big-name artists, like Missy Elliott, Jazze Pha (pronounced Jazzie Fay), Petey Pablo, and R. Kelly.

The song "Goodies" made it to the top of the Billboard 100 and stayed there for seven whole weeks. Not many new artists can reach this level of popularity so fast. The entire album did well too. It reached number three on the Billboard Chart its first week. It sold more than two million copies and was nominated for four Grammys. A Grammy is an industry-wide award for musicians that is similar to an Oscar for actors. Being nominated for a Grammy is a huge honor. To be nominated for four Grammys for your first album is extremely impressive.

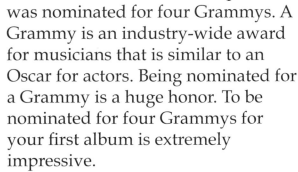

Not only did Goodies get Ciara Grammy nominations, it also helped her win other awards.

Not only did *Goodies* get Ciara Grammy nominations, it also helped her win other awards. Since 2004, she has received three Teen Choice Awards and two Black Entertainment Awards. She was honored with two MTV Video Music Awards and a Vibe Award. In 2005, she received the Sammy Davis Jr. Award and was named Soul Train's Female Entertainer of the Year. And then in 2006, she won her first Grammy — for "Lose Control," which she had performed with Missy Elliott.

Ciara's music is upbeat and has a great rhythm. Many people like to dance to it. It is written in a style that many people call Crunk & B. This style of music is both "crazy" and "funky." Lil' Jon and his group are known as the Kings of Crunk. Since *Goodies* was the first Crunk & B album released by a woman, people started calling Ciara the First Lady of Crunk & B. Ciara isn't so sure she likes this title, though. As she has told reporters, "It was never a fitting title.

On September 7, 2005, Ciara proudly displayed the awards she received during the 10th Annual Soul Train Lady of Soul Awards ceremony.

It was so funny because when people would call me that, I had so many different sounds and types of songs. It just didn't make sense in the big picture."

So who exactly is this young artist named Ciara? Just a year before stardom, she was a cheerleader in high school. Now, she is a famous musician with her own CDs. How did someone so young become so famous so fast? Ciara knew how to make it all happen—with hard work and sacrifice. She learned at a young age that if you want anything out of your life, you have to work hard for it.

Ciara's story doesn't end here. And it doesn't start here either. Ciara's story starts much earlier, in 1985, on a military base in Texas.

Hip-Hop Hooray for Her Highness

*T*he year 1985 was an important one for Carleson and Jackie Harris. On October 25, they welcomed their new little baby daughter into the world. This was the couple's first child, and they wanted to give her a special name. They decided on Ciara Princess Harris.

Ciara was the name of a popular Revlon perfume from the 1970s. It had a beautiful fragrance that smelled like raspberry, lemon, rosewood, and jasmine. Carleson and Jackie felt that this was a perfect name for their new baby. Their little girl deserved a name as beautiful as she was.

Ciara was born in the state capital of Texas, but she didn't get to stay in Austin for very long. Both of her parents had careers in the United States military. Her father served in the Army, and her mother was in the Air Force. During Ciara's childhood, the Harris family moved from one military base to another. Besides Texas, they lived in many places in the United States, including Nevada, Arizona, California, and New York. The Harris family even lived for a time on a U.S. military base in Germany.

It was hard for Ciara to move around so much. Just when she had made some friends and settled into school, her parents would get transferred to a new place and she'd have to start all over again. Any kid who has moved around a lot can relate to how Ciara must have felt. It's hard when you're always the new kid on the block. Even so, having a childhood like this made Ciara stronger. She learned how to make friends quickly and to say goodbye to people she cared about when she had to leave. She also learned how to adapt to new situations and make herself happy wherever she was.

Even though Ciara moved around a lot, she always tried to become involved in school activities. She started cheerleading when she was eight years old. She loved it. She enjoyed performing in front of people and entertaining them. Believe it or not, Ciara actually considers herself a shy person. The more she performed in front of people, though, the easier it has become for her. "I have to tell myself that this is what I do and I can't be shy," Ciara says. "I've gained more confidence as I've grown."

> *Even though Ciara moved around a lot, she always tried to become involved in school activities.*

During her youth, Ciara also discovered that she was a very talented runner. At most of the schools she attended, she was a member of the track team. She competed in many races and brought home lots of ribbons and medals to display in her room.

When Ciara was in her early teens, her parents finally decided to make a permanent home for their family. They

Ciara happily signs an autograph during an Atlanta Hawks game. She simply adores her fans.

found a nice place in the suburbs of Atlanta, Georgia. Now, the Harris family could settle into their new life.

Ciara was very happy about her new situation. She could relax and make friends—and keep them for a long time. She could also get more involved in school activities, since she knew she wouldn't be leaving in the middle of the year. Ciara jumped into her new life in Atlanta with both feet.

The family settled in a town called Riverdale, which is only fourteen miles south of downtown Atlanta. First, Ciara attended North Clayton High School. Then she attended Riverdale High, eventually graduating in 2003. She enjoyed attending both of these schools.

Ciara considers her hometown to be Riverdale, Georgia. She was given the key to the city on October 19, 2006.

Once again, Ciara shone in school activities. In the athletic arena, she became a star on the school's track team. She also continued performing and entertaining as a cheerleader. As a member of the squad, she was known for her impressive dance skills. When the squad performed its routines and stunts, Ciara was a base. This is one of the most important positions in cheerleading. The bases are the people at the bottom of the pyramid who support the other girls. They also help other cheerleaders do jumps in the air and catch them when they come back down. Only the strongest members of the squad are allowed to be bases.

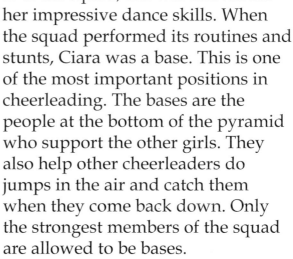

Ciara quickly became one of the school's most popular students. Her weekends were generally packed with one social activity after another.

Ciara worked hard to be the best cheerleader she could be. Her efforts paid off. As a senior, she was selected as the captain of her varsity squad.

Ciara quickly became one of the school's most popular students. Her weekends were generally packed with one social activity after another. She hung out with her friends at the roller rink and at dance parties. She also attended the prom, sporting events, and other school functions. Just about everyone seemed to like her and wanted to be her friend.

CHAPTER 3

A Girl with Ambition

*T*hroughout her youth, Ciara enjoyed doing many different types of activities. She loved dancing, running, cheering, and hanging out with her friends. But there is one activity that she loved to do more than anything: singing. Ciara started singing songs that she heard on the radio when she was just a little girl. She'd jam to the music as she performed in front of her bedroom mirror. She'd belt out her favorite tunes in the shower every morning. She'd even buzz around the house singing her latest favorite ballad until her mother would have to tell her to hush.

When Ciara was fourteen years old, she decided to start setting short-term and long-term goals for herself. She had a long list of things she wanted to accomplish with her life, and she felt that the best way to accomplish these things was to set goals.

One day when she was home from school, she watched Destiny's Child perform on television. She was captivated by the group's performance. She knew instantly what one of her goals had to be. She wanted to get a major record deal and be a famous musician just like the women in Destiny's Child!

Becoming a famous musician probably sounds like something any fourteen-year-old would want to do. But Ciara wasn't just an ordinary fourteen-year-old with a dream. Ciara had ambition. She was determined to make her dream a reality. She knew she couldn't just set this goal and then sit back and do nothing to make it happen. That would be like saying she wanted to be an astronaut but then never learning anything about science. Ciara knew that if she wanted her dreams to come true, she would have to make a plan for herself. Once she had her plan, she would have to work hard and never give up on her dream.

Ciara knew that if she wanted her dreams to come true, she would have to make a plan for herself.

Ciara was plenty busy with her friends and school activities. She barely had time in her day for those things, let alone add anything else to it. She had to make a decision. If she really wanted to become a famous entertainer, she would have to give up some other things in her life. She decided to break up with her boyfriend and spend less time hanging out with her friends. She cut out movies and parties and limited her phone time. This was a hard decision to make, but she was willing to sacrifice some fun now in order to make her dreams come true.

Ciara knew she couldn't just sing in the shower and in front of the mirror and be magically discovered as a musician. If she wanted to be signed by a major record company, she would have to start performing in public.

Even though Ciara is a shy person at heart, she still loves performing for her fans.

Ciara works on a recording of "We Are Family" at the Chalice Recording Studios, Los Angeles, in 2005. Artists spend many hours in the studio recording their music.

Ciara started singing anywhere and everywhere she could. She performed in community and school talent shows. She sang the national anthem at sporting events. Every time she performed, she pretended that a big music executive was in the audience. That way, she always did the best job she could. She never knew how or when her big break might come.

Not only did Ciara start singing in public, she also started spending more time writing her own music. She didn't want to just sing the songs that other people had written. She wanted to sing music of her own. She knew that the only way her music would ever be good enough was to spend time on it consistently. "It was all about being patient and making my craft the best it could be," Ciara says. "I was working on my music for four long years. I really invested a lot of time and hard work."

> *She knew that the only way her music would ever be good enough was to spend time on it consistently.*

When Ciara was fifteen, she joined an all-girl group called Hearsay. This trio performed mainly rhythm and blues, or R&B, music. Other famous musicians who sing this type of music include Ashanti, Boyz II Men, and Usher.

Hearsay did not become famous like these other groups did. The group performed at various places in and around Atlanta for small crowds. But after only six months, the three girls decided to go their separate ways.

To most people, having your first music group break up this quickly might have seemed like a big disappointment, but it was all okay with Ciara. She no longer wanted to be part of a group. She wanted to focus her attention on a solo career. She picked up right where she left off and continued writing music and performing on her own.

Dreams Can Come True

*C*iara's big break came when she was a senior in high school. One day, the former manager of Hearsay contacted Ciara and wanted to introduce her to Jazze Pha. He was one of the biggest names in Atlanta's music industry. Ciara was very excited. She couldn't believe she was actually going to meet this famous producer. He had his own record label, Sho'nuff, and had helped people like Aliyah (uh-LEE-uh) and Toni Braxton become famous. Maybe he could do the same thing for her!

Ciara and Jazze Pha hit it off instantly. He was impressed by her talent and her ambition. Ciara felt like she had a lot in common with this artist and even called him her "musical soul mate." After working with Ciara for only five days, Jazze Pha signed her to his record label. Ciara had met one of her first goals.

Ciara faced another important decision. She would have to devote most of her time to fulfilling her new record contract. She would no longer have time for cheerleading. "I loved cheerleading so much," she told a magazine reporter in 2005. "But it was very compromising for me to do

Ciara combines her singing and dancing talents into an energetic performance on stage.

cheerleading and music. I had to sacrifice cheer for my music career. It was very hard for me to do because I was so happy as captain, but it was definitely worth it. [Music is] my career, my life."

> *She spent hours and hours working on her first album, which would be called Goodies. She wanted everything to be just perfect on it.*

Ciara quit the squad and jumped into her music career. She spent hours and hours working on her first album, which would be called *Goodies*. She wanted everything to be just perfect on it. Ciara was fortunate to work with many talented artists on this album.

After *Goodies* was released, Ciara started touring the country. She performed on many television shows, including *Live with Regis and Kelly*, *The Tonight Show with Jay Leno*, and *Ellen: The Ellen Degeneres Show*. In 2006, Ciara performed in concerts in Washington, D.C.; Chicago; Seattle; Las Vegas; New York City; Park City, Utah; and her hometown of Atlanta.

In the summer of 2006, Ciara was also in an MTV movie called *All You've Got*. She played the part of Becca Watley. The movie was about a high school girls' volleyball team. Ciara really enjoyed her first acting job. She felt like she had a lot in common with her character, Becca. First, much like Ciara was in high school, Becca was the "queen bee" of her school. She was very athletic and was the star of the volleyball team. Second, Becca struggled with figuring out what to do with her life. Of course, Ciara knew how that felt too. Third, in the film, Becca gets upset that her parents rarely come to her games. Many kids can relate to

On June 28, 2005, Ciara performed at the Black Entertainment Television Awards in Hollywood, California. She was nominated for four awards that evening.

this. Parents have busy schedules and it's hard for them to come to everything. Ciara's parents had tried to watch her in as many things as they could, but they still missed some events that were important to her. With so much in common with her character in this film, it really wasn't that difficult for Ciara to play the part.

Ciara's second album, *Ciara: The Evolution*, was released in December 2006. Ciara wrote or cowrote most of the songs on it. Some of the most popular ones include "Like a Boy," "Promise," and "Get Up." The album sold an impressive 338,000 copies during the first week, causing it to land at number one on the Billboard chart.

Ingredients for Success

*C*iara has often been compared to Janet Jackson and Aliyah. She has also been called the "female version of Usher." She feels like these are all great compliments because she respects these artists. Yet Ciara isn't trying to be someone else. "I do feel like we're all different," she says. "People will say, 'She's trying to be like her,' but I'm saying to myself, like, 'I'm trying to do me.' " She hopes that people will remember her as Ciara, not as a copycat of someone else.

Ciara has many role models. She hopes to run her business career, as P. Diddy has run his. She respects Oprah Winfrey and Michael Jordan for what they have been able to achieve with their lives. She also admires Michael Jackson for his talent as an entertainer. In 2005, she worked with Jackson on "I Have This Dream," a single that would benefit victims of Hurricane Katrina.

Just like many celebrities, Ciara doesn't like to talk about her personal life. For nearly a year, she dated musician Bow Wow. When they broke up, many reporters tried to find out why, but Ciara just didn't want to talk about it. This is understandable. Not many people would want to talk about

Most young girls only dream about becoming a famous recording artist.
Ciara not only dreamed it, she worked hard to achieve it.

a breakup. It is sometimes too painful. Plus it's not really anyone else's business to know.

Yet Ciara does tell reporters a few details about her life. She says that she likes being single right now. It gives her time to focus on her goals and her music career. Some reporters have asked her if she would ever date a famous guy again. Ciara believes there is more to a person than that. She says, "If you're a great person and you're a confident man and you're a really sweet guy—and you have it all together and you just so happen to be a celebrity, it is what it is. If you have all those characteristics and you're a doctor, it is what it is."

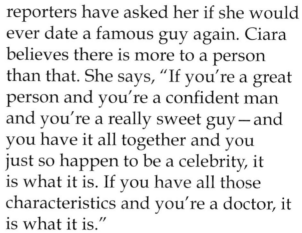

Ciara is involved in every aspect of her career. She writes, cowrites, and produces the songs on her albums.

Now that Ciara has achieved her first short-term goal—getting a record deal—she has started to set new ones. "I want to sell more and more millions of records and make more great music videos," she says. She also wants to start her own record label someday.

Ciara is involved in every aspect of her career. She writes, cowrites, and produces the songs on her albums. She makes up the dance numbers for her videos and performances. She also helps come up with ideas to advertise and market her image. And she gets involved in the accounting part of her career by making sure she knows how and where her money is being spent.

As anyone who has watched Ciara perform knows, she is a very talented dancer. She has been moving and grooving to music since she could walk. Ciara wanted to share her love of

Ciara achieved great success with her first album, Goodies. *Within nine months of its release, it was certified double platinum — meaning it sold over two million copies.*

dancing with others. She decided to open up a dance agency in Atlanta. At this studio, called Universal Dance Studio, teens can come and learn the latest dance-club moves.

Ciara loves fashion. She has a unique style and someday wants to start her own fashion line. She also hopes to model her own clothing designs on the runways. At a fashion show in New York in 2006, Ciara told reporters, "It reminded me of how much of a model I want to be. I look forward to the day I can walk out on the runway with a really dope outfit."

Ciara has big dreams for her future career. Her dream is "to be a successful businesswoman, and the ultimate, ultimate goal is to become a billionaire." She told newspaper reporters in 2006, "I used to say I wanted to be a combination of P. Diddy and Oprah, and I'll call that person Poprah."

On the other hand, Ciara knows that she has already achieved many great things with her life so far. If that's all that comes true for her, she says, that will be enough. "It's good to know that whenever I look back on my career, I can say that my first single was number one on the Hot 100 Billboard Chart. That's a blessing to me," she told a *Teen Tribute* reporter in 2005.

Ciara also says, "In life, you determine your destiny. No one around you will get you to where you want to be but you."

Ciara has a lot of advice for young people who want to be successful and live their dreams. First, she says, "make the right decisions for you, even if they mean sacrifice." It was very difficult for Ciara to give up cheerleading when she signed her record contract. It was also very sad when she had to spend less time doing fun things with her friends so that she could practice her music. She was willing to make those sacrifices in order to fulfill her dreams.

Ciara also says, "In life, you determine your destiny. No one around you will get you to where you want to be but you." Third, she says to "just try new things, and you can always do something that you don't expect to do." Sometimes doing this is hard. But, like Ciara says, "You have to just put yourself out there and try new things. That's what it's all about."

She would be trying yet another new thing in the summer of 2007. She was chosen to star in a film adaptation of the musical *Mama, I Want to Sing!* R&B powerhouse Patti LaBelle and actress Lynn Whitfield would also star. Although this was not Ciara's first acting job, it was her first major movie role. Looking forward to the challenge, she said, "I'm thinking, 'Ciara's gonna go in, she's gonna go hard, she's gonna challenge herself, she's gonna knock it out.' "

Ciara also says that "one of the most important ways to accomplish what you want is to have goals and have a plan." Ciara definitely knows about goals. She started setting them as a young teen and she continues to set them even to this day.

Ciara says the fifth piece of advice she has for young people is to "most importantly, stay focused. The sky is the limit." Ciara never takes her eye off her goals, and she suggests that all young people do the same. Once you have set your goal, you should work very, very hard to accomplish it. And never give up on your dreams.

What's great about Ciara's advice is that she knows it really does work. She did all these things when she was a teen, and it helped her dream come true. If you follow in her footsteps, a world of possibilities could open for you too!

> *Ciara also says that "one of the most important ways to accomplish what you want is to have goals and have a plan."*

1985	Ciara Princess Harris is born in Austin, Texas, on October 25.
Early 1990s	The Harris family settles down in Riverdale, Georgia.
1993	Ciara becomes a school cheerleader.
1999	She sets a goal to become a recording artist. She starts singing in talent shows and at sporting events.
1999– 2003	Ciara attends North Clayton and Riverdale High Schools; she becomes a track star, a member of cheer-leading squad, and serves as cheerleading captain.
2000	She is part of the R&B girl-group Hearsay.
2002	Jazze Pha signs her to his record label Sho'nuff.
2003	She graduates from Riverdale High School in Riverdale, Georgia.
2004	*Goodies* is released on September 28; Ciara appears on *Regis and Kelly*; she appears on *Tonight Show with Jay Leno*; and she performs on *Dick Clark's New Year's Rockin' Eve*.
2005	Ciara receives the Sammy Davis Jr. Entertainer Award; is on an episode of Ashton Kucher's MTV show *Punk'd*; sings on the *Coach Carter* sound track; receives Teen Choice Awards for "Oh" with Ludacris and "1, 2 Step" with Missy Elliott; receives Black Entertainment Television Awards; the DVD *Ciara Goodies: The Videos and More* is released in July; tours with Bow Wow and Chris Brown in "We Ain't Done Yet Holiday Jam."
2006	With Missy Elliott, Ciara wins her first Grammy for "Lose Control"; she appears in her first acting role in MTV movie *All You've Got*; *Ciara: The Evolution* is released in December.
2007	She performs at New Orleans Essence Music Festival in July; is nominated for three BET Awards; is chosen as MTV's First Lady; appears on *Vibe* and *Giant* magazine covers; announces she will star in *Mama, I Want to Sing*, a movie with Patti LaBelle and Lynn Whitfield.

Albums

2006 *Ciara: The Evolution*

2004 *Goodies*

Hit Singles

2006 "So What" Field Mob featuring Ciara
      "Get Up" with Chamillionaire
      "Promise"

2005 "1, 2 Step" with Missy Elliott
      "Oh" with Ludacris
      "Lose Control" Missy Elliott featuring Ciara
      "Like You" Bow Wow featuring Ciara

2004 "Goodies"

Articles

Bliss, Karen. "She's Got the Goods." *Teen Tribute*. Spring 2005, p. 26.

"Ciara Aims for Fluidity." *Quad-City Times*. December 17, 2006.

"Ciara Previewing *Evolution* on Tour." *Billboard*. October 10, 2006.

Walker, Melissa. "Ciara Says." *American Cheerleader*. August 2005, pp. 29–30

FURTHER READING

Works Consulted

"Ciara Is What She Is: Talented and Ambitious." *LA Daily News*. December 14, 2006.

Carlson, Erin. "Ciara Just Herself." *PE.com: Southern California News*. December 11, 2006.

———. "Ciara Proves Her Staying Power with Second Hit Album." *Arizona Daily Star*. December 13, 2006.

———. "Ciara's Modest Goal: Become Larger Than Life." *Orlando Sentinel*. December 9, 2006.

———. "Ciara's Not Stopping at *Goodies*." *The [Raleigh, NC] News & Observer*. December 12, 2006.

———. "Ciara to Star in 'Mama, I Want to Sing!' " *Associated Press*. June 1, 2007. http://www.wtopnews.com/index. php?nid=114&sid=1156008

Jones, Steve. "Versatile Ciara Evolves as Songwriter." *USA Today*. December 5, 2006.

Knopper, Steve. "Evolution Is Next Step for Ciara." *[New York] Newsday*. December 7, 2006.

Lee, Chris. "Ciara Feels the Magic with Evolution." *Los Angeles Times*. December 26, 2006.

———. "Yeah, Ciara Saw All of This Coming." *Los Angeles Times*. December 16, 2006.

Lee, Elysa. "Ciara." *InStyle*. May 2005, p. 296.

Mitchell, Gail. "Ciara." *Billboard*. January 29, 2005, p. 15.

———. "Now, Hear This . . . Ciara." *Billboard*. September 28, 2004, p. 48.

Ogunnaike, Lola. "One Name, Many Goals for a Driven R&B Star." *The New York Times*, December 6, 2006.

"Pretty Young Thing: Ciara." *Giant Magazine*. November 27, 2006.

"R&B/Hip-Hop Artist Ciara Steals the #1 Billboard Spot,"
   Rap News Direct, December 14, 2006,
   http://www.rapnewsdirect.com/0-202-262251-00.html
"R&B Singer Ciara." *People*. October 18, 2004, p. 132.
"The Rising Star." *Atlanta*. May 2006, p. 89.
Tardio, Andres. "Ciara on Love, Children and 50 Cent." *Hip
   Hop News*. March 8, 2007.
   http://www.hiphopdx.com/index/news/id.4965/title.
   ciara-on-love-children-and-50-cent
Venable, Malcolm. "Ciara." *Interview*. May 2004, p. 52.
"The Wise Guide." *Nashua Telegraph*. December 10, 2006.
World Entertainment News Network, "Michael Jackson
   Charity Single Featuring Snoop Dogg, R. Kelly, Ciara and
   Others To Be Released Soon," February 22, 2006, http://
   www.starpulse.com/news/index.php/2006/02/22/
   michael_jackson_charity_single_featuring/

On the Internet

CiaraWorld. Ciara's Official Website.
   http://www.ciaraworld.com
MTV.com. "Ciara." http://www.mtv.com/bands/c/ciara/
   news_feature041104/
MTV.com. "Ciara Talks Single Life, Dreams of Acting Like a
   Boy on Evolution." http://www.mtv.com/news/
   articles/1541563/20060922/ciara.jhtml
MTV.com. "Ciara Knocks out Gwen, Eminem's Crew to Take
   Top Billboard Spot." www.mtv.com/news/
   articles/1547891/20061213/ciara.jhtml
MTV.com. "Ciara: The Queen Bee of the Little Madonnas."
   www.mtv.com/movies/news/
   articles/1513522/11112005/story.jhtml
Billboard.com. "Ciara Biography." http://www.billboard.com/
   bbcom/bio/index.jsp?pid=617021

INDEX